CW00429673

B1 ENGLISH
Questions & Answers

For Indefinite Leave to Remain and British Citizenship

ISBN: 9798875951169

Introduction 4

How to Prepare 5

Dictionaries 8

Verbs for Ability, Permission, and Requests 11

Comparative and Superlative Adjectives 13

Countable and Uncountable Nouns 13

Present Simple and Continuous Tenses 14

Past Simple and Continuous Tenses 15

Future Tenses: Will and Going To 16

Prepositions of Time, Place, and Movement 17

Daily Life and Routine 18

Exercise: Reflect on Your Routine 19

Work and Education 19

Exercise: Fill in the Gaps (Part 1) 21

Exercise: Fill in the Gaps (Part 2) 23

Exercise: Fill in the Gaps (Part 3) 25

Exercise: Fill in the Gaps (Part 4) 27

Exercise: Fill in the Gaps (Part 5) 29

Reading Comprehension Exercise 31

Reading Comprehension Answers 34

Conversational English Questions and Answers 35

Introduction

Welcome to "B1 English Questions and Answers for Indefinite Leave to Remain and British Citizenship." This essential guide is your gateway to achieving two key goals in your UK settlement journey – securing Indefinite Leave to Remain (ILR) and ultimately, British citizenship.

This book marks the start of a transformative adventure, one that equips you with vital language skills to confidently approach the ILR and citizenship application process. We're not just focusing on meeting the B1 English language requirement; our goal is to enhance your fluency and assurance in everyday English communication.

Embarking on the path to ILR and British citizenship is an exhilarating, yet demanding quest. It extends beyond mere formalities; it's about showcasing your dedication to being an active and contributing member of British society. English proficiency is crucial in this journey, unlocking opportunities and fostering meaningful interactions in your new community.

Within these pages, you'll discover an array of resources, practical activities, and insightful guidance to bolster your language skills. We'll navigate you through the nuances of the B1 English test, offer strategies for effective language acquisition, and provide you with the means to express yourself eloquently in diverse scenarios.

This book is designed for learners at various stages – whether you're starting your English language journey or refining your existing abilities. With commitment and regular practice, you'll not only meet the language prerequisites but also embrace English as a key instrument for integration and accomplishment in the UK.

Embark on this enriching journey with us, as we help lay the foundations for your prosperous future in the United Kingdom.

Your aspiration to obtain Indefinite Leave to Remain and British citizenship begins here – with the mastery of B1 English.

How to Prepare

1. Grammar: A strong command of grammar is crucial. Ensure your sentences adhere to proper structure and follow grammatical rules. There are abundant resources available for grammar practice, both online and in textbooks.

2. Listening: Hone your listening skills by exposing yourself to various English accents and dialects. Watch English-language films, TV shows, and news broadcasts. Regular engagement with spoken English will sharpen your listening abilities.

3. Vocabulary: Expanding your vocabulary is essential. Pay attention to the words used in books, newspapers, and online articles. Cultivate a habit of reading English materials regularly. Mindmaps can assist you in

exploring synonyms, antonyms, and related words, enriching your lexicon.

4. Pronunciation: Clear and accurate pronunciation is pivotal for effective communication. Practice articulating words and sounds correctly. Observe the accents and intonations of native English speakers. It's acceptable to have an accent, but prioritize clarity and attentiveness to articulation.

5. Fluent Speaking: Work towards speaking fluently and confidently. Strive for concise and lucid sentences, avoiding excessively intricate structures that may lead to confusion. In case you forget a word, remain composed; use expressions like "Just a moment" or "One second, please" to grant yourself time to recollect it. If the word escapes you, acknowledge it and proceed.

6. Accuracy: While perfection is not mandatory, aim for precise and accurate communication. Ensure your word choices and grammar convey your intended meaning. Extensive reading can enhance your grammatical accuracy.

Language Practice Tips:

- Engage in conversations with native speakers within your family or community. Interacting with them will provide invaluable practice opportunities.

- Dedicate at least 20 minutes each day to watching English-language programs you enjoy. This will not only enhance your listening skills but also expose you to everyday conversations.

Test-Specific Preparation:

If you reside in the UK and are working here, chances are you already possess a B1 level of proficiency. Nevertheless, do not underestimate the significance of thorough preparation. Even if you are proficient at this level, overlooking specific criteria important to the examiner can impact your performance.

Vocabulary Range:

To excel, concentrate on everyday words and phrases rather than overly specialized terms related to your profession or hobbies. Keep it simple and universal. Mindmaps can be a valuable tool for expanding your range of words.

Pronunciation:

Practice clear pronunciation to ensure your words are understood on the first attempt. Some allowances are made for accents, particularly for non-native speakers. Pay close attention to native speakers and the emphasized sounds and intonation.

The King's English:

For the examination, aim for a clear and neutral pronunciation, often referred to as "Received Pronunciation" or the King's English. This is the standard for formal situations, and all audio in the exam will employ this accent. However, in real-life situations, you may adapt to regional accents based on your surroundings.

Speaking Fluency:

Strive for fluent and coherent speech. Utilize simple and familiar sentence structures, and minimize excessive complexity. Brief pauses to gather your thoughts are acceptable, but protracted pauses should be avoided.

Accuracy and Corrections:

While perfection is not obligatory, clarity of meaning is essential. If you make an error, promptly correct it. This is a common practice among native speakers.

Dictionaries

A dictionary goes beyond being a mere reference book; it emerges as a potent tool capable of significantly enhancing your language proficiency and delving deeper into the meanings of words. Whether you're a language enthusiast or an adept wordsmith, mastering the art of efficient dictionary use is a valuable skill that can unveil new avenues of communication and knowledge.

Here's a guide to becoming proficient in the art of using a dictionary effectively:

1. Choose the Appropriate Dictionary:
Select a dictionary that aligns with your requirements.
Various types are available, including monolingual
(explaining words in the language you're learning),
bilingual (providing translations), and specialised
dictionaries (focused on particular subjects like law,
science, or literature). Your purpose and language
proficiency level should guide your choice.

2. Understand the Structure:
Familiarise yourself with the dictionary's layout. Entries
are generally arranged alphabetically, featuring each
word alongside its pronunciation, part of speech (noun,
verb, adjective, etc.), definitions, and sample sentences.
Proficiency in this format will facilitate efficient
navigation.

3. Decode Pronunciations:
Pay attention to pronunciation guides, often utilising
systems like the International Phonetic Alphabet (IPA) or
diacritical marks. Learning how to interpret these
symbols will enable you to pronounce words accurately.

4. Grasp Varied Meanings:
Numerous words possess multiple meanings depending
on context. Carefully peruse the different definitions
offered to capture the subtleties of a word's usage.
Example sentences prove particularly useful in
illustrating these nuances.

5. Explore Synonyms and Antonyms:
Dictionaries often include lists of synonyms (words with
similar meanings) and antonyms (words with opposite

meanings). These can broaden your vocabulary and aid in expressing yourself with precision.

6. Employ Example Sentences:
Sample sentences showcase words in their contextual usage. They provide valuable insights into word application, word combinations that frequently occur, and grammatical structures. Studying these sentences will enrich your comprehension.

7. Delve into Etymology:
Certain dictionaries provide insights into a word's origin or etymology. Uncovering the history of words can make them more memorable and assist in drawing connections between different languages.

8. Cross-Reference and Explore:
Don't restrict yourself to a single word entry. Dictionaries often include cross-references to related words, idioms, and phrases. Seize the opportunity to explore and expand your linguistic knowledge.

9. Hone Pronunciation:
Utilise the pronunciation guide to practice pronouncing words aloud. This practice will elevate your oral skills and contribute to a more fluent speaking style.

10. Maintain a Vocabulary Journal:
- Keep a vocabulary journal where you note down new words, their meanings, and sample sentences. Regularly revisiting and using these words will reinforce your learning.

11. Digital Dictionaries and Language Apps:
- Consider using digital dictionaries and language learning apps, which frequently offer supplementary features such as audio pronunciation, interactive exercises, and offline access.

12. Context Is Crucial:
- Always bear in mind that a word's meaning can shift based on the context in which it is used. Take context into account when interpreting definitions and example sentences.

Mastering the use of a dictionary transcends mere word comprehension; it immerses you in the language, broadens your vocabulary, and nurtures a deeper appreciation for the beauty of words. With practice and an inquisitive spirit, you'll discover that a dictionary can be your trusted companion on your linguistic journey, guiding you towards language mastery one word at a time.

Verbs for Ability, Permission, and Requests

Modal verbs like "can," "could," "may," and "might" assume a vital role in expressing one's ability, seeking permission, and making requests. Each modal verb carries its unique level of formality and nuance, rendering them versatile instruments in language use.

For Ability:
- "Can" and "could" are frequently employed to describe someone's capability to accomplish tasks. "Can" pertains

to present ability (e.g., "She can speak three languages"), while "could" often refers to past abilities or a less certain present ability (e.g., "In my youth, I could run exceptionally fast" or "Could you perhaps assist me with this?").

For Permission:
- "Can" and "may" serve the purpose of requesting or granting permission. "Can" is informal (e.g., "Can I borrow your pen?"), while "may" is more formal and courteous (e.g., "May I be excused from the table, please?"). When granting permission, "can" is commonly used (e.g., "You can leave once you finish your homework").

For Requests:
- "Could" and "would" are often employed for making polite requests. "Could" is considered slightly more polite or indirect than "can" (e.g., "Could you kindly pass me the salt, please?"), and "would" is reserved for highly polite requests, particularly in formal settings (e.g., "Would you be so kind as to provide me with the report?").

Comprehending the nuanced distinctions between these modal verbs is essential for effective communication. They enable individuals to express themselves clearly and appropriately in a variety of social contexts, be they informal or formal. Proficiency in the usage of modal verbs significantly enhances one's ability to articulate capabilities, seek permissions, and make requests with the desired level of politeness and precision.

Comparative and Superlative Adjectives

Comparative Adjectives come into play when comparing two entities or individuals. They frequently take the "-er" form or are prefaced by "more" for longer adjectives. For instance, "taller" in "She is taller than her brother," or "more beautiful" in "This painting is more beautiful than that one." Comparatives establish a relationship of superiority, inferiority, or equality (employing 'as...as') between two entities.

Superlative Adjectives are utilised to depict the utmost or highest degree of a quality when comparing three or more entities. Typically, these adjectives end with "-est" or are introduced by "most" for longer adjectives. For instance, "the tallest" in "She is the tallest in her class," or "the most beautiful" in "This is the most beautiful painting in the gallery." Superlatives pinpoint one entity that surpasses or falls below all others in a group.

Both comparative and superlative adjectives must harmonise with the nouns they modify concerning number, gender, and definiteness. They serve as indispensable tools for effective communication, providing a succinct and lucid manner to compare and contrast diverse entities. Proficiency in these forms enriches language expression, permitting more nuanced and precise descriptions and comparisons.

Countable and Uncountable Nouns

Countable Nouns denote objects, individuals, or things that can be counted. They have both singular and plural forms, with the singular often preceding 'a' or 'an,' and the plural frequently concluding with '-s' or '-es'. For example, "apple/apples" or "car/cars." Countable nouns can be quantified using numbers and words such as many, few, several, etc., responding to the question "How many?" For instance, "I have three books."

Uncountable Nouns (or mass nouns) pertain to substances, concepts, or collective categories of things that cannot be counted as individual units. They lack a plural form and cannot be accompanied by 'a' or 'an'. Examples encompass "water," "sand," "information," and "advice." These nouns are quantified using words like much, little, a lot of, some, etc., answering the question "How much?" For instance, "I need some water."

Present Simple and Continuous Tenses

The Present Simple Tense serves as a tool for describing habitual actions, timeless general truths, and facts. It's the preferred tense for discussing routines and permanent situations. For instance, when we say, "She reads books every evening," we are highlighting a regular habit. Similarly, when we state, "The sun rises in the east," we are presenting a general truth. Typically, this tense involves using the base form of the verb, with the addition of 's' or 'es' for third-person singular subjects.

On the other hand, the Present Continuous Tense is utilised to indicate actions currently unfolding at the time of speaking or temporary situations. It conveys ongoing actions and is constructed using the present tense of 'to be' (am/is/are) followed by the '-ing' form of the verb. For example, "She is reading a book right now," suggests that the action is occurring in the present moment. It is also employed for future plans or arrangements, as in, "I am meeting a friend tomorrow."

Past Simple and Continuous Tenses

The Past Simple Tense is primarily employed to narrate completed actions that transpired at a specific point in the past. It offers a straightforward way to recount events with a distinct beginning and end. For instance, "She visited Paris last summer," communicates a completed action that occurred at a definite time in the past. The construction of the Past Simple typically involves adding '-ed' to regular verbs (walked, talked) and using the second form of irregular verbs (saw, went).

In contrast, the Past Continuous Tense centres on ongoing actions in the past, often at a particular moment. It is used to establish a scene, describe simultaneous actions, or indicate an action that was interrupted by another. The tense is formed using the past tense of 'to be' (was/were) followed by the '-ing' form of the verb. For example, "She was reading a book when I called," highlights an ongoing action (reading) that was interrupted by another action (calling). It is valuable for portraying a past scenario, such as, "It was raining all evening."

Future Tenses: Will and Going To

The future tenses in English, specifically "will" and "going to," hold significance in discussing events or actions yet to occur, each with distinct purposes and conveying unique nuances.

"Will" is frequently employed when making a spontaneous decision at the time of speaking or for promises, offers, and predictions. It is formed by simply using 'will' followed by the base form of the verb. For example, "I will call you tomorrow," signifies a decision made in the present moment. It is also utilised for predictions based on personal opinions or beliefs, as in, "I think it will rain later."

In contrast, "going to" is used for future plans or intentions that have been decided before the present moment and for predictions based on current evidence. This tense is constructed by using 'am/is/are' + 'going to' + the base verb. For instance, "She is going to start a new job next week," implies a pre-arranged plan. In terms of predictions, "going to" is employed when there is present evidence supporting the prediction, as in, "Look at those dark clouds; it's going to rain."

The choice between "will" and "going to" often depends on the context and the speaker's perspective. While "will" leans towards spontaneity or uncertainty, "going to" is employed for more definite plans or predictions based on visible evidence. Comprehending the nuances between these two future forms is crucial for mastering expressions related to the future in English.

Prepositions of Time, Place, and Movement

Prepositions constitute fundamental components of English grammar, furnishing essential insights into the connections between nouns or pronouns and other elements within sentences. Prepositions specifically tailored to denote time, place, and movement serve as pivotal tools for indicating when, where, and how actions unfold.

Prepositions of Time encompass terms like "at," "on," and "in," elucidating the temporal aspects of events. "At" pinpoints precise moments (e.g., at 5 o'clock), "on" designates days and dates (e.g., on Monday, on July 4th), and "in" delineates longer durations such as months, years, decades, or seasons (e.g., in April, in 2023, in the 1990s, in winter). Each preposition defines a specific timeframe for the occurrence or activity.

Prepositions of Place elucidate the location of objects or actions. Common prepositions of place encompass "in," "on," and "at." "In" is employed for enclosed spaces (e.g., in a room, in a building), "on" denotes a surface (e.g., on the table), and "at" identifies a specific point (e.g., at the door, at the station). These prepositions serve to precisely identify an object's or person's whereabouts.

Prepositions of Movement delineate the direction of an object or person's motion. They encompass terms like "to," "from," "up," "down," "over," "under," "into," and "out of." "To" signifies movement towards a designated destination (e.g., go to the office), "from" denotes the starting point (e.g., depart from home), while "into" and "out of" elucidate motion into or away from enclosed spaces (e.g., walk into a room, emerge out of a building).

Daily Life and Routine

Every individual follows a unique daily regimen. A typical day often commences with the jarring sound of an alarm clock. For many, mornings entail a brisk shower, followed by a nourishing breakfast. Breakfast selections frequently encompass cereal, toast, eggs, or fruit, with some opting for a reviving cup of coffee or tea.

Subsequent to breakfast, the ensuing step often involves heading to work or school. This journey might entail catching a bus, driving, or perhaps a brief stroll. At work or school, the day is generally occupied with an array of tasks or lessons. Lunch breaks furnish an opportunity to relax and savour a meal, often comprising a sandwich, salad, or a similar repast.

As the afternoon ensues, the focus pivots towards completing work or educational assignments. After the workday culminates, many individuals partake in leisure activities, be it reading, exercising, or indulging in television. Dinner assumes a significant role in the evening, as it represents a time for families to convene, relish a meal together, and share anecdotes about their day. Popular dinner options encompass pasta, meat, vegetables, or occasionally a simple soup.

Before retiring for the night, some individuals adhere to a routine encompassing activities such as checking emails, preparing for the following day, or embarking on a skincare regimen. Ultimately, it is time for slumber, a period of restorative repose in preparation for the day ahead.

Exercise: Reflect on Your Routine

How does your daily routine compare? Write a brief paragraph delineating your typical day, incorporating select vocabulary and phrases from this passage.

Work and Education

Work and education constitute substantial facets of many individuals' lives. The educational journey often initiates with primary school, subsequently progressing to secondary education. Post this phase, certain students opt for university or vocational training programmes. Educational institutions offer an array of subjects, spanning mathematics and science to the arts and languages. University attendees typically specialise in a specific discipline, such as engineering, medicine, or business.

Within the realm of employment, an extensive array of job types and industries exists. Individuals engage in diverse work settings, encompassing offices, factories, or outdoor environments. Office workers frequently dedicate their day to tasks performed on computers, which may entail creating reports or responding to emails. Factory employees might participate in the manufacturing of products. Occupations requiring outdoor engagement include roles such as construction workers or farmers.

The work environment varies considerably. Some vocations necessitate collaborative efforts, while others are characterised by independence. Many individuals experience a blend of both. Apart from the core tasks, employees may participate in meetings, training sessions, and performance evaluations.

Work and education encompass more than just earning an income or acquiring knowledge; they also provide opportunities for social interaction and the development of interpersonal skills. Both spheres contribute significantly to personal growth and play pivotal roles in society.

Exercise: Fill in the Gaps (Part 1)

Complete the following sentences with the appropriate words or phrases:

1. I _____ (work) at this company for five years.
2. She _____ (read) a book when I called her.
3. My best friend and I _____ (know) each other since we were children.
4. The weather is nice today, so we _____ (go) for a walk in the park.
5. They _____ (not watch) TV very often.
6. If you _____ (have) any questions, feel free to ask me.
7. I'll _____ (visit) my grandparents next weekend.
8. The cat is sleeping, so please _____ (be) quiet.
9. I _____ (study) Spanish because I want to travel to Spain next year.
10. We _____ (not eat) sushi before, but we'd like to try it.

Answers:
1. have been working
2. was reading
3. have known
4. are going
5. do not watch
6. have
7. visit
8. be
9. am studying
10. have not eaten

would not let her go, saying nothing, merely assuming that Bethan would stay with him. She nodded absently. What did it matter? As they moved over the floor, he would come close and then draw away, but each time the gap narrowed between them until his arms came to circle her and she pulled herself easily away. It was a game. The next time, his hands settled tightly on her waist to lift her into the air, only to be gently returned to the flagstones. The last steps were taken from the rear, and she could feel the warmth of his breath on the back of her neck as he crushed her too closely against him. In spite of herself, she felt her heart begin to race and a deep blush invade her cheeks. There was something about this man . . . but she would not be used again by some courtly rogue. Not again!

Abruptly she pushed his arms away, protesting, 'How dare you, sir! I think you presume too much!'

'Do I, Bethan? In that case, you are to blame.'

His voice. She felt her breath stop, shaking in her throat. He lifted his mask so that she could see his face, but still she said nothing.

'Yes, you are to blame, Bethan, too lovely for your own good.' Hugh let his eyes pass over her delightfully concealed face. He had known her from the first, as he would know her anywhere.

'It is not I who am to blame, sir, it is you; and other men like you who only take without giving . . .' Why did he always loosen her tongue in this way? Why, just this last time, could he not be kind?

'Is that what you think of me? A greedy womaniser—is that what you think, Bethan?'

She could not speak, afraid that her words would be the wrong ones.

'Well, of course you are quite right . . .' he said slowly.

There was anger now. He was worse than the King with his ill-concealed arrogance—as if he were proud of it!

'You are beyond words, Hugh D'Savoury! Indeed, I wish I had never set eyes on you!' Yet she still wanted him, even as his fierce eyes swept insolently over her and a smile came to rest infuriatingly on his beautiful mouth.

'That is a pity, since I am sure that at various times I have given you some meed of pleasure, or are you too proud to admit it?'

Up came her eyes in outraged disbelief, and he saw how her lips quivered, saw how the full breasts swelled and rose so temptingly as she drew a furious angry breath.

'You are beneath contempt—insufferable! A great brutish oaf who knows nothing of women!' There were a thousand insults she wanted to throw at him, but none seemed vile enough to wound him, and there was that mocking smile on his mouth again.

Suddenly her attention was taken by another, who had come up beside her, and his great shadow fell across Hugh's gilded doublet like a warning. 'Enough, Hugh! Your jesting goes too far.'

Bethan shifted her angry gaze to the other man, and met the eyes of the King. The breath seemed to stop in her lungs. She was dwarfed by him, and her knees grew weak as she endeavoured to give a trembling, clumsy curtsy.

'Well, is it done?' he asked impatiently.

Exercise: Fill in the Gaps (Part 2)

Complete the following sentences with the appropriate words or phrases:

1. I usually _____ (have) breakfast at 7:00 AM.
2. _____ (you / visit) any interesting places recently?
3. Sarah _____ (work) as a nurse for three years now.
4. They _____ (not go) to the gym very often, but they want to start.
5. My brother _____ (play) the guitar in a band.
6. She _____ (study) French because she loves the language.
7. We _____ (not see) that movie yet.
8. The children _____ (swim) in the pool when it started raining.
9. I'm looking forward to _____ (travel) to Italy next summer.
10. Can you please _____ (pass) the salt?

Answers:
1. have breakfast
2. Have you visited
3. Sarah has been working
4. do not go
5. plays
6. studies
7. have not seen
8. were swimming
9. traveling
10. pass

Exercise: Fill in the Gaps (Part 3)

Complete the following sentences with the appropriate words or phrases:

1. My grandmother _____ (live) in the same house for over fifty years.
2. They _____ (not eat) pizza often, but they love it.
3. Sarah _____ (practice) the piano every evening.
4. He _____ (not like) coffee, so he always orders tea at the café.
5. We _____ (plan) a trip to the mountains next month.
6. My cat _____ (sleep) on the couch right now.
7. Tom and his sister _____ (play) tennis every Sunday morning.
8. I _____ (visit) the art museum last weekend.
9. Can you _____ (pass) me the salt, please?
10. The children _____ (swim) in the lake when we arrived.

Answers:
1. has lived
2. do not eat
3. practices
4. does not like
5. are planning
6. is sleeping
7. play
8. visited
9. pass
10. were swimming

Exercise: Fill in the Gaps (Part 4)

Complete the following sentences with the appropriate words or phrases:

1. She _____ (study) for her exams at the moment.
2. My parents _____ (live) in the same house since they got married.
3. _____ (you / watch) any good movies lately?
4. The weather is nice, so we _____ (go) for a walk in the park.
5. I _____ (not speak) Spanish, but I want to learn.
6. They _____ (not visit) their relatives often, but they enjoy it when they do.
7. My friend _____ (play) the piano beautifully.
8. Last summer, we _____ (travel) to France and Italy.
9. Can you please _____ (bring) me a glass of water?
10. The children _____ (build) a sandcastle on the beach right now.

Answers:
1. is studying
2. have lived
3. Have you watched
4. are going
5. do not speak
6. do not visit
7. plays
8. traveled
9. bring
10. are building

Exercise: Fill in the Gaps (Part 5)

Complete the following sentences with the appropriate words or phrases:

1. I _____ (read) a fascinating book last night.
2. Mary _____ (work) as a teacher for five years.
3. _____ (you / play) any musical instruments?
4. He _____ (not like) spicy food, so he orders mild dishes.
5. We _____ (plan) to visit the museum next weekend.
6. My dog _____ (sleep) on the couch right now.
7. Jim and his brother _____ (practice) basketball every Saturday morning.
8. I _____ (visit) my grandparents last summer.
9. Could you please _____ (pass) the salt?
10. The kids _____ (swim) in the pool when it started raining.

Answers:
1. read
2. has worked
3. Do you play
4. does not like
5. are planning
6. is sleeping
7. practice
8. visited
9. pass
10. were swimming

Reading Comprehension Exercise

Title: "The Great Barrier Reef"

Read the following passage and answer the questions that follow:

The Great Barrier Reef is the world's largest coral reef system, located in the Coral Sea off the coast of Queensland, Australia. It stretches over 2,300 kilometers and is made up of thousands of individual reefs and islands. This natural wonder is so large that it can even be seen from space!

The Great Barrier Reef is home to a diverse range of marine life, including colorful coral formations, various species of fish, sharks, sea turtles, and many other fascinating creatures. It is a popular destination for snorkelers and scuba divers from all over the world who come to explore its vibrant underwater world.

In addition to its incredible biodiversity, the Great Barrier Reef also plays a vital role in the world's ecosystem. The coral reefs provide a habitat for marine species, protect the coastline from erosion, and even help with climate regulation by absorbing carbon dioxide from the atmosphere.

Despite its beauty and importance, the Great Barrier Reef faces several threats, including coral bleaching caused by rising ocean temperatures, pollution from coastal development, and overfishing. Conservation efforts are underway to protect and preserve this magnificent natural wonder for future generations.

Now, answer the following questions:

Where is the Great Barrier Reef located?
a) Off the coast of New Zealand
b) In the Caribbean Sea
c) In the Coral Sea off the coast of Queensland, Australia
d) In the Indian Ocean

How long is the Great Barrier Reef?
a) 230 kilometers
b) 1,000 kilometers
c) 2,300 kilometers
d) 5,000 kilometers

What kind of marine life can be found in the Great Barrier Reef?
a) Only sharks and sea turtles
b) Only fish and sharks
c) A diverse range of marine life including colorful coral formations, various species of fish, sharks, sea turtles, and more
d) Only colorful coral formations

What role does the Great Barrier Reef play in the world's ecosystem?
a) It has no significant role in the ecosystem
b) It provides a habitat for land animals
c) It helps with climate regulation by releasing carbon dioxide

d) It provides a habitat for marine species, protects the coastline, and helps with climate regulation by absorbing carbon dioxide from the atmosphere.

What are some of the threats to the Great Barrier Reef?
a) Overpopulation of marine species
b) Rising ocean temperatures, pollution, and overfishing
c) Climate change and volcanic eruptions
d) None of the above

Reading Comprehension Answers

Where is the Great Barrier Reef located?
Answer: c) In the Coral Sea off the coast of Queensland, Australia

How long is the Great Barrier Reef?
Answer: c) 2,300 kilometers

What kind of marine life can be found in the Great Barrier Reef?
Answer: c) A diverse range of marine life including colorful coral formations, various species of fish, sharks, sea turtles, and more

What role does the Great Barrier Reef play in the world's ecosystem?
Answer: d) It provides a habitat for marine species, protects the coastline, and helps with climate regulation by absorbing carbon dioxide from the atmosphere.

What are some of the threats to the Great Barrier Reef?
Answer: b) Rising ocean temperatures, pollution, and overfishing

Conversational English Questions and Answers

Question: What do you usually do on weekends?
Answer: On weekends, I usually relax at home and sometimes meet my friends. We often go to the cinema or have lunch together.

Question: Can you describe your hometown?
Answer: My hometown is a small, peaceful town surrounded by hills. It has a few shops, a park, and a beautiful river running through it.

Question: What's your favourite type of weather and why?
Answer: I love sunny weather because it's perfect for outdoor activities. I enjoy going for walks and feeling the warmth of the sun.

Question: How do you get to work or school?
Answer: I usually take the bus to get to work. It's convenient and allows me to read during the journey.

Question: What kind of food do you like and why?
Answer: I'm fond of Italian cuisine, especially pasta. I like it because it's tasty and there are so many different varieties to try.

Question: Have you read any interesting books recently?
Answer: Yes, I recently read a mystery novel called "The Missing Piece". It was really intriguing and kept me guessing until the end.

Question: What do you think are the benefits of learning a new language?
Answer: Learning a new language opens up many opportunities. It allows you to communicate with more people and understand different cultures better.

Question: Could you tell me about a memorable holiday you've had?
Answer: Last year, I visited Paris. It was memorable because of the beautiful sights, like the Eiffel Tower and the Louvre. The food was amazing too!

Question: What are your hobbies and how did you start them?
Answer: My hobbies are painting and cycling. I started painting in school and cycling as a way to explore my local area.

Question: What's an important lesson you've learned in life?
Answer: An important lesson I've learned is to always be patient. Good things take time, and it's important not to rush through life.

Question: How often do you exercise and what activities do you do?
Answer: I exercise about three times a week. I usually go jogging in the park and sometimes attend a yoga class.

Question: What's your favourite holiday and why?
Answer: My favourite holiday is Christmas because it's a time when my family comes together. We enjoy decorating the house and exchanging gifts.

Question: Do you prefer reading books or watching films? Why?
Answer: I prefer reading books because they allow me to use my imagination more. Also, I find them relaxing, especially before bedtime.

Question: Can you tell me about a traditional dish from your country?
Answer: A traditional dish from my country is shepherd's pie. It's made with minced lamb and vegetables, topped with mashed potatoes.

Question: What are the advantages of living in a city?
Answer: Living in a city has many advantages, like having easy access to shops, restaurants, and cultural activities. There's always something to do.

Question: How do you like to spend a rainy day?
Answer: On a rainy day, I enjoy staying indoors, perhaps with a good book or watching a film. Sometimes I bake something sweet.

Question: What subject did you enjoy most at school and why?
Answer: I enjoyed English the most because I love reading and writing stories. It was always fascinating to learn about different authors and their styles.

Question: Have you ever traveled to another country? What was it like?

Answer: Yes, I've traveled to Spain. It was wonderful, especially because of the sunny weather, beautiful beaches, and delicious food.

Question: What's an important skill you've learned outside of school or work?
Answer: An important skill I've learned is cooking. It's not only useful but also a fun way to be creative and try new recipes.

Question: If you could learn a new hobby, what would it be and why?
Answer: I would like to learn photography. Capturing moments and beautiful landscapes seems like a rewarding and enjoyable hobby.

Question: What's your favourite season and why?
Answer: My favourite season is spring because the weather starts to get warmer, and the flowers begin to bloom. It's very picturesque.

Question: Do you have any pets? Can you describe them?
Answer: Yes, I have a dog named Max. He's a golden retriever with a shiny coat and friendly nature. He loves playing fetch.

Question: What did you do on your last birthday?
Answer: On my last birthday, I had a small party with my family. We had a barbecue in our garden and a delicious chocolate cake.

Question: What's your favourite kind of music and why?

Answer: I enjoy listening to pop music because it's upbeat and makes me feel happy. I especially like songs with catchy melodies.

Question: What is a typical breakfast in your country?
Answer: A typical breakfast in my country includes toast, eggs, and bacon. Some people also like to have a bowl of cereal or porridge.

Question: Have you ever been to a concert? What was it like?
Answer: Yes, I went to a rock concert last year. It was amazing! The energy of the crowd and the live music made it an unforgettable experience.

Question: What do you usually do to relax after a busy day?
Answer: To relax, I usually read a book or take a long bath. Sometimes, I also do some meditation to unwind.

Question: Can you tell me about a famous person from your country?
Answer: A famous person from my country is J.K. Rowling, the author of the Harry Potter series. She's known worldwide for her creative writing.

Question: What are your plans for the next holiday?
Answer: For the next holiday, I plan to visit the seaside. I'm looking forward to relaxing on the beach and swimming in the sea.

Question: Why is learning English important to you?

Answer: Learning English is important to me because it's a global language. It helps me communicate with people from different countries and opens up more job opportunities.

Question: What's your favourite way to spend a weekend?
Answer: My favourite way to spend a weekend is going for a hike in the countryside. It's refreshing and a great way to exercise.

Question: Can you describe a book you have recently read?
Answer: I recently read a book called "The Light Between Oceans". It's a touching story about a lighthouse keeper and his wife, set on a remote island.

Question: What do you think is the best way to stay healthy?
Answer: I think the best way to stay healthy is to maintain a balanced diet and regular exercise. Also, getting enough sleep is very important.

Question: How do you prefer to travel, by car or by train? Why?
Answer: I prefer to travel by train because it's less stressful than driving. I can read or relax, and I don't have to worry about traffic.

Question: What's a popular festival in your country?
Answer: A popular festival in my country is Bonfire Night on November 5th. People light bonfires and set off fireworks to remember Guy Fawkes.

Question: Do you enjoy cooking? What's your best dish?

Answer: Yes, I enjoy cooking. My best dish is spaghetti carbonara. It's simple but delicious, and my family loves it.

Question: What was the last movie you saw? Did you like it?
Answer: The last movie I saw was "Dune". I really liked it because of its impressive visuals and intriguing plot.

Question: What are some popular sports in your country?
Answer: In my country, football is very popular. Cricket and rugby are also widely followed and played by many people.

Question: Do you have a favourite quote or saying? What is it?
Answer: Yes, my favourite quote is "Life is what happens when you're busy making other plans" by John Lennon. It reminds me to enjoy the present.

Question: What's your favourite childhood memory?
Answer: My favourite childhood memory is going to the beach with my family every summer. We would build sandcastles and swim in the sea.

Question: What kind of movies do you like and why?
Answer: I like comedy movies because they make me laugh and relax. My favourite is "Bridget Jones's Diary" because it's so humorous.

Question: Do you play any musical instruments? Which one?
Answer: Yes, I play the guitar. I've been playing for about five years now, and I really enjoy it, especially playing songs with friends.

Question: What's your favourite way to spend time with your family?
Answer: My favourite way to spend time with my family is having a picnic in the park. It's nice to enjoy the outdoors and have a casual meal together.

Question: Do you prefer summer or winter sports? Give an example.
Answer: I prefer summer sports, like swimming. I love being in the water on a hot day, and it's a great way to stay fit.

Question: How do you celebrate New Year's Eve in your country?
Answer: In my country, we usually celebrate New Year's Eve with fireworks and parties. Many people also have a special dinner with their family.

Question: What's the most interesting place you've visited?
Answer: The most interesting place I've visited is Rome. The historical sites like the Colosseum and the Roman Forum were fascinating.

Question: Can you describe a traditional celebration in your country?
Answer: A traditional celebration in my country is the May Day festival. We have maypole dancing, and there are lots of spring-themed decorations.

Question: What do you think is the most important invention of the last century?

Answer: I think the internet is the most important invention. It has completely changed how we communicate and access information.

Question: What are your plans for your next holiday?
Answer: For my next holiday, I'm planning to go hiking in the Lake District. I've heard the scenery is beautiful, and I enjoy outdoor activities.

Question: Do you like to try new foods? What's the most unusual thing you've eaten?
Answer: Yes, I like trying new foods. The most unusual thing I've eaten is sushi when I visited Japan. It was different but very tasty.

Question: What's your favourite hobby and why do you enjoy it?
Answer: My favourite hobby is gardening because it's relaxing and rewarding to see the plants grow. I also enjoy being outdoors.

Question: Can you tell me about a memorable trip you took?
Answer: A memorable trip I took was to Scotland. The landscapes were breathtaking, and I loved exploring the historic castles.

Question: What do you like most about living in your city?
Answer: What I like most about living in my city is the mix of culture and history. There are great museums and lively markets.

Question: What's your favourite type of restaurant and why?
Answer: My favourite type of restaurant is Italian because I love pasta and pizza. The atmosphere is usually cosy and inviting too.

Question: What do you think is the best way to learn a new language?
Answer: I think the best way to learn a new language is through immersion – speaking with native speakers and practising regularly.

Question: What's your favourite public holiday and how do you celebrate it?
Answer: My favourite public holiday is Christmas. I celebrate it with my family, and we enjoy a special meal and exchange gifts.

Question: Can you describe a traditional outfit or costume from your country?
Answer: A traditional outfit from my country is the kilt, usually worn in Scotland. It's a knee-length skirt with a tartan pattern.

Question: What was the last book you read and would you recommend it?
Answer: The last book I read was "The Night Circus" by Erin Morgenstern. I would recommend it for its imaginative story and beautiful writing.

Question: Do you have any plans for the weekend?

Answer: Yes, this weekend I'm going to a local art exhibition. I'm looking forward to seeing some modern art pieces.

Question: What's an important cultural event in your country?
Answer: An important cultural event in my country is the Notting Hill Carnival. It's a vibrant festival celebrating Caribbean culture with music and dance.

Question: How do you usually spend your evenings?
Answer: I usually spend my evenings relaxing at home. I often watch TV or read a book, and sometimes I cook a nice dinner.

Question: What's your favourite outdoor activity?
Answer: My favourite outdoor activity is cycling. I love exploring different paths and enjoying the fresh air.

Question: Can you tell me about a hobby you'd like to start?
Answer: I'd like to start photography. Capturing beautiful moments and sceneries seems really exciting and a great way to express creativity.

Question: What's the most interesting historical place you've visited?
Answer: The most interesting historical place I've visited is the Tower of London. It has a fascinating history and it's amazing to see the old architecture.

Question: Do you prefer reading fiction or non-fiction? Why?

Answer: I prefer reading fiction because it allows me to escape into different worlds and experiences. I love the creativity and imagination in stories.

Question: What's a typical weekend activity for people in your country?
Answer: A typical weekend activity in my country is going for a walk in the park or having a barbecue if the weather is nice.

Question: What was your favourite subject in school and why?
Answer: My favourite subject in school was history. I found it interesting to learn about different events and cultures from the past.

Question: Have you ever tried a sport you found really challenging?
Answer: Yes, I tried rock climbing once. It was challenging but also very thrilling. I enjoyed the physical and mental challenge.

Question: What's a popular TV show or series in your country right now?
Answer: A popular TV show in my country right now is a detective series called "Mystery Lane." It's very suspenseful and has great characters.

Question: How do you like to celebrate special occasions with your friends or family?
Answer: I like to celebrate special occasions by having a meal together. Whether it's at home or in a restaurant, it's nice to share good food and conversation.

Question: What's your favourite form of exercise?
Answer: My favourite form of exercise is swimming. I find it relaxing and it's a great full-body workout.

Question: Can you describe a memorable event from your childhood?
Answer: A memorable event from my childhood was my first trip to the seaside. I remember building sandcastles and playing in the waves.

Question: What's a popular dish in your country?
Answer: A popular dish in my country is fish and chips. It's typically served wrapped in paper and eaten with salt and vinegar.

Question: Do you enjoy team sports or individual sports more? Why?
Answer: I enjoy individual sports more, like running. It gives me time to clear my head and I can set my own pace.

Question: What's the most interesting city you've visited?
Answer: The most interesting city I've visited is Edinburgh. It has a great mix of history, culture, and beautiful architecture.

Question: What's your preferred way to travel on holiday?
Answer: My preferred way to travel on holiday is by train. I enjoy watching the scenery pass by and it's more relaxing than driving.

Question: Have you ever attended a live sports event? What was it like?
Answer: Yes, I attended a football match once. The atmosphere was electric with all the fans cheering and singing.

Question: What's a hobby you've always wanted to try but haven't yet?
Answer: I've always wanted to try pottery. It looks like a fun and creative way to make something unique.

Question: What's a book that had a significant impact on you?
Answer: A book that had a significant impact on me is "To Kill a Mockingbird" by Harper Lee. It opened my eyes to issues of justice and morality.

Question: How do you usually celebrate your birthday?
Answer: I usually celebrate my birthday with a small gathering of friends and family. We have dinner together and sometimes go out to a favourite spot.

Question: What's your favourite way to spend a holiday?
Answer: My favourite way to spend a holiday is by visiting new places. I love exploring different cultures and trying local food.

Question: Can you describe your dream job?
Answer: My dream job would be working as a wildlife photographer. I love nature and capturing it through photography would be amazing.

Question: What's a skill you'd like to learn this year?

Answer: This year, I'd like to learn how to bake. I've always enjoyed cooking, and baking seems like a fun challenge.

Question: What's the best movie you've seen recently?
Answer: The best movie I've seen recently is "The Grand Budapest Hotel." I loved its unique style and humour.

Question: Do you have a favourite author? Who is it and why?
Answer: My favourite author is Jane Austen. I love her writing style and the way she developed characters and social commentary in her novels.

Question: How do you prefer to spend a rainy day?
Answer: On a rainy day, I prefer to stay indoors, maybe curl up with a good book or watch a film with a cup of tea.

Question: What's the most interesting place in your hometown?
Answer: The most interesting place in my hometown is the old castle. It's full of history and has a beautiful view of the surrounding area.

Question: What type of music do you listen to when you want to relax?
Answer: When I want to relax, I listen to classical music. It's soothing and helps me to unwind after a long day.

Question: Can you tell me about a festival or event that is unique to your country?
Answer: A unique event in my country is the Highland Games in Scotland. It includes traditional sports like caber tossing and showcases Scottish culture.

Question: What do you usually do to stay focused when working or studying?
Answer: To stay focused, I make sure to take regular short breaks. I also listen to instrumental music to help me concentrate.

Question: What's your preferred mode of transport for daily commuting?
Answer: I prefer cycling for daily commuting. It's environmentally friendly and a good form of exercise.

Question: Can you describe an interesting tradition in your family?
Answer: An interesting tradition in my family is that we gather for a large brunch on New Year's Day. It's a great way to start the year together.

Question: What's a hobby you've recently taken up?
Answer: I've recently started learning to play the piano. It's challenging, but I enjoy learning to play new songs.

Question: What's a memorable book you've read this year?
Answer: A memorable book I've read this year is "The Alchemist" by Paulo Coelho. Its message about following your dreams really resonated with me.

Question: Do you have a favourite type of international cuisine?
Answer: My favourite type of international cuisine is Japanese. I love sushi and ramen for their flavours and presentation.

Question: How do you like to spend time outdoors?
Answer: I enjoy hiking in the mountains. It's a great way to experience nature and get some exercise.

Question: What's an interesting historical site you've visited?
Answer: An interesting historical site I've visited is Stonehenge. The mystery and history behind it are really fascinating.

Question: What genre of movies do you prefer and why?
Answer: I prefer science fiction movies because they explore imaginative and futuristic concepts, which I find intriguing.

Question: Can you tell me about a celebration or holiday that's important in your country?
Answer: An important holiday in my country is Remembrance Day. It's a day to honour and remember military members who have served in wars.

Question: What strategies do you use to manage stress?
Answer: To manage stress, I practice yoga and meditation regularly. They help me stay calm and maintain a balanced mindset.

Question: What's a recent hobby you've started and why?
Answer: I recently started birdwatching. It's fascinating to learn about different bird species and it's a peaceful activity.

Question: Can you describe a local festival or event in your area?

Answer: A local event in my area is the annual food festival. It features dishes from various local restaurants and live music performances.

Question: What's your favourite way to relax on a weekend?
Answer: My favourite way to relax on a weekend is by going for long walks in the countryside. It's quiet and the scenery is beautiful.

Question: Have you ever tried a sport that you found particularly challenging?
Answer: Yes, I tried snowboarding last winter. It was challenging to balance at first, but it was a lot of fun once I got the hang of it.

Question: What's a memorable gift you've received?
Answer: A memorable gift I received was a handmade photo album from a close friend. It was filled with photos and notes from our adventures together.

Question: How do you celebrate major achievements?
Answer: I celebrate major achievements by having a nice dinner with my family and friends. It's a great way to share the happiness.

Question: What's a book or movie that made a significant impact on you?
Answer: A book that made a significant impact on me is "The Power of Now" by Eckhart Tolle. It changed my perspective on living in the present moment.

Question: Do you have a favourite place to visit in your country?
Answer: Yes, my favourite place to visit is the Lake District. It's peaceful, and the landscapes are stunning.

Question: Can you describe an interesting custom from your culture?
Answer: An interesting custom from my culture is the tea drinking ceremony. It's a traditional practice that involves a precise and mindful way of making tea.

Question: What's your approach to learning new things?
Answer: My approach to learning new things is to start with the basics and practice regularly. I also find it helpful to learn from others and ask questions.

Question: What's a typical weekend activity for you?
Answer: A typical weekend activity for me is going to the local market. I enjoy browsing the stalls and buying fresh produce.

Question: Can you describe your favourite piece of clothing?
Answer: My favourite piece of clothing is a blue denim jacket. It's comfortable, stylish, and goes well with almost everything.

Question: What's an interesting tradition or custom from your country?
Answer: An interesting tradition in my country is the celebration of Midsummer. It involves lighting bonfires and dancing around a maypole.

Question: Have you ever participated in a team sport? Which one?
Answer: Yes, I've played on a football team. It was a great experience for teamwork and staying active.

Question: What's a film that you can watch over and over again?
Answer: A film I can watch repeatedly is "The Lord of the Rings." I love the epic story and the stunning scenery.

Question: How do you usually spend time with your friends?
Answer: I usually spend time with my friends by having a meal together or going to see a movie. Sometimes we just hang out and chat at someone's house.

Question: What's the most interesting place you've studied or worked at?
Answer: The most interesting place I've worked at was a small bookshop in my town. It had a quaint charm and a great selection of books.

Question: Do you have a favourite childhood memory? What is it?
Answer: My favourite childhood memory is going on family camping trips. We would roast marshmallows and tell stories around the campfire.

Question: What's a skill or hobby you're currently improving?
Answer: I'm currently improving my cooking skills. I've been trying out new recipes and techniques, which has been really fun.

Question: How do you like to celebrate special occasions?
Answer: I like to celebrate special occasions by gathering with family and friends, sharing a meal, and enjoying each other's company.

Question: What's your favourite thing to do on a rainy day?
Answer: On a rainy day, I love to curl up with a good book and a cup of tea. It's so cosy and relaxing.

Question: Can you tell me about a local delicacy from your region?
Answer: A local delicacy in my region is Cornish pasties. They're pastry filled with meat and vegetables, traditionally eaten by miners.

Question: What's an interesting fact about your country's history?
Answer: An interesting fact about my country's history is that it was the birthplace of the industrial revolution, which dramatically changed society.

Question: Do you have any plans for your next vacation?
Answer: For my next vacation, I'm planning to visit the Scottish Highlands. I'm looking forward to the scenic hikes and historic castles.

Question: What's a recent positive experience you've had?
Answer: A recent positive experience I had was attending a friend's wedding. It was a beautiful ceremony and great to catch up with old friends.

Question: How do you stay motivated when learning something new?
Answer: To stay motivated, I set small, achievable goals and remind myself of the benefits of learning. Celebrating progress helps too.

Question: What's a typical breakfast like in your country?
Answer: A typical breakfast in my country includes toast, eggs, bacon, and tea. Some people also enjoy a bowl of cereal or fruit.

Question: Can you describe a festival that you enjoy attending?
Answer: I enjoy attending the Notting Hill Carnival. It's vibrant, full of music and dance, and celebrates Caribbean culture.

Question: What's your favourite way to exercise?
Answer: My favourite way to exercise is by going for a run in the park. It clears my mind and I enjoy the fresh air.

Question: How do you like to spend your free time?
Answer: In my free time, I like to paint. It's a creative outlet for me and I find it very therapeutic.

Question: What's your favourite type of weather and why?
Answer: My favourite type of weather is sunny but not too hot. It's perfect for spending time outdoors without feeling uncomfortable.

Question: Can you describe a memorable celebration or party you attended?

Answer: I attended a memorable birthday party last year on a boat. We sailed along the river, and the view of the city at night was stunning.

Question: What's a book you've read recently that you would recommend?
Answer: I recently read "The Kite Runner" by Khaled Hosseini. It's a powerful story about friendship and redemption that I would highly recommend.

Question: Do you have a favourite place to relax in your city or town?
Answer: Yes, there's a quiet park near my home where I love to relax. It has a small lake and is perfect for reading or just enjoying nature.

Question: What's a skill you've learned recently?
Answer: I've recently learned basic carpentry. I made a small bookshelf, which was both challenging and rewarding.

Question: What's the most interesting documentary you've watched?
Answer: The most interesting documentary I watched recently was about the deep sea. It showed some incredible creatures and landscapes I had never seen before.

Question: What's a traditional dish from your country that you love?
Answer: A traditional dish I love is Sunday roast. It's a hearty meal with roasted meat, potatoes, vegetables, and gravy.

Question: Can you tell me about a hobby you enjoy with friends or family?
Answer: I enjoy hiking with my family. We explore different trails, and it's a great way to spend time together and stay active.

Question: What's a memorable trip you've taken in your country?
Answer: A memorable trip I took was to the Lake District. The landscape was breathtaking, and I enjoyed the peaceful walks and charming villages.

Question: How do you usually celebrate your birthday?
Answer: I usually celebrate my birthday with a small dinner party at home with family and close friends. I prefer intimate gatherings.

Question: What's your favourite way to spend time with family?
Answer: My favourite way to spend time with my family is having a barbecue in our backyard. It's casual and fun, and everyone enjoys it.

Question: Can you describe a hobby that you find unusual or interesting?
Answer: An unusual hobby I find interesting is geocaching. It's like a treasure hunt using GPS, and it takes you to places you might never have seen otherwise.

Question: What's a memorable movie you've seen recently?

Answer: I recently watched "The Grand Budapest Hotel." It was memorable for its unique storytelling and colourful visuals.

Question: Do you have a favourite place to visit for relaxation?
Answer: Yes, my favourite place for relaxation is the beach. I love the sound of the waves and the feeling of sand under my feet.

Question: What's a skill you'd like to master?
Answer: I'd like to master cooking. I can make basic dishes, but I'd love to learn how to cook more complex and varied meals.

Question: What's the most exciting sporting event you've attended or watched?
Answer: The most exciting sporting event I've watched was a live football match between two top teams. The atmosphere in the stadium was electric.

Question: Can you tell me about a traditional celebration in your country?
Answer: A traditional celebration in my country is Guy Fawkes Night on November 5th. We have fireworks and bonfires to remember the Gunpowder Plot.

Question: What's a hobby you enjoy that helps you relax?
Answer: A hobby that helps me relax is knitting. It's soothing and I get a sense of accomplishment from creating something.

Question: Can you describe an interesting local landmark?

Answer: An interesting local landmark is the ancient castle on the hill. It has a great view of the city and a lot of history.

Question: How do you prefer to spend a quiet evening at home?
Answer: On a quiet evening at home, I prefer to listen to music or watch a documentary. It's a nice way to unwind and learn something new.

Question: What's your favourite local restaurant and why?
Answer: My favourite local restaurant is a small Italian place downtown. They have the best homemade pasta and a very cosy atmosphere.

Question: Can you describe a memorable event from your school days?
Answer: A memorable event from my school days was when our class put on a play. I had a small part, but the whole experience of rehearsing and performing was really fun.

Question: What's a typical dish that people eat in your country?
Answer: A typical dish in my country is roast beef and Yorkshire pudding. It's especially popular on Sundays.

Question: Do you prefer reading physical books or e-books? Why?
Answer: I prefer reading physical books. I enjoy the feel of the paper and the experience of turning the pages. Plus, I like seeing them on my bookshelf.

Question: What's the best concert or live performance you've ever attended?
Answer: The best concert I've ever attended was by a famous rock band in a large outdoor stadium. The energy was incredible, and the music was unforgettable.

Question: How do you like to spend your time on a day off?
Answer: On a day off, I like to go for a long bike ride in the countryside. It's relaxing and a great way to enjoy nature.

Question: Can you tell me about a popular tourist attraction in your country?
Answer: A popular tourist attraction in my country is the British Museum in London. It has a vast collection of art and artefacts from all over the world.

Question: What's a hobby you think might be interesting to start?
Answer: I think starting a garden could be an interesting hobby. It would be rewarding to grow my own vegetables and herbs.

Question: Can you describe an interesting piece of art you've seen?
Answer: I once saw an incredible modern art installation that was an entire room filled with colourful lights. It was like walking through a rainbow.

Question: What's your favourite way to exercise?
Answer: My favourite way to exercise is swimming. It's a full-body workout, and I find the water to be very calming.

Question: What's a book you've read that left a strong impression on you?
Answer: A book that left a strong impression on me is "1984" by George Orwell. It made me think deeply about freedom and society.

Question: Can you describe a traditional holiday or festival in your culture?
Answer: In my culture, we celebrate Diwali, the festival of lights. We light candles, set off fireworks, and share sweets with family and friends.

Question: What's a place in your city or town that you like to visit?
Answer: I enjoy visiting the botanical gardens in my city. It's peaceful, and I love seeing all the different plants and flowers.

Question: Do you have a favourite sport or physical activity?
Answer: My favourite physical activity is yoga. It helps me stay flexible and relaxes my mind.

Question: What's a recent movie you watched and enjoyed?
Answer: I recently watched "The Shape of Water" and really enjoyed it. The storytelling and visuals were fantastic.

Question: How do you usually celebrate your birthday?
Answer: I usually celebrate my birthday by having a dinner with family and close friends. I prefer quiet celebrations.

Question: Can you tell me about a unique tradition from your country?
Answer: A unique tradition from my country is the tea ceremony. It's a ceremonial way of preparing and drinking tea, focusing on mindfulness and aesthetics.

Question: What's your favourite type of international cuisine?
Answer: My favourite type of international cuisine is Mexican. I love the flavors and the variety of dishes like tacos and enchiladas.

Question: Can you describe a memorable trip you took?
Answer: A memorable trip I took was to the Grand Canyon. The views were breathtaking, and the hiking trails were both challenging and exciting.

Question: What's a hobby or skill you'd like to learn in the future?
Answer: I'd like to learn photography in the future. Capturing moments and beautiful landscapes seems like a rewarding skill to have.

Question: What's your preferred method of transportation for long distances?
Answer: For long distances, I prefer taking the train. It's comfortable and I can enjoy the scenery along the way.

Question: Can you tell me about a special family tradition?
Answer: In our family, we have a tradition of having a big family reunion every summer. We all gather at my grandparents' house for a weekend of food and fun.

Question: What's your favourite indoor activity?
Answer: My favourite indoor activity is playing board games. It's a great way to spend time with friends and family.

Question: Do you have a favourite local café or coffee shop? What makes it special?
Answer: Yes, there's a small coffee shop near my place that I love. They have a cozy atmosphere and the best homemade cakes.

Question: What's an outdoor activity you enjoy in the winter?
Answer: In the winter, I really enjoy skiing. It's exhilarating to glide down the slopes and enjoy the snowy landscape.

Question: How do you prefer to spend your evenings?
Answer: I usually spend my evenings reading or watching a series on TV. It's a nice way to relax after a day's work.

Question: Can you describe a festival that's important in your culture?
Answer: An important festival in my culture is Holi, the festival of colors. We celebrate it by throwing colored powder at each other and it symbolizes joy and the arrival of spring.

Question: What's a hobby that keeps you active?
Answer: A hobby that keeps me active is dancing. I take salsa classes weekly, which is not only fun but also a great workout.

Question: Can you describe a memorable experience you had while traveling?
Answer: A memorable experience I had while traveling was snorkeling in the Great Barrier Reef. Seeing the vibrant marine life up close was incredible.

Question: What's a skill or hobby you've always wanted to try and why?
Answer: I've always wanted to try pottery. I think shaping clay into something useful seems both artistic and therapeutic.

Question: What's an unusual food you've tried and liked?
Answer: An unusual food I've tried and liked is sushi. I was hesitant at first, but I really enjoyed the fresh taste and unique textures.

Question: Can you describe a memorable concert or live show you've attended?
Answer: I attended a memorable concert by a famous pop artist last year. The energy was incredible, and the live music experience was unforgettable.

Question: What's a book genre you typically enjoy? Can you give an example?
Answer: I typically enjoy mystery novels. One of my favourites is "Sherlock Holmes" by Arthur Conan Doyle, with its intriguing plots and characters.

Question: Do you have a favourite outdoor spot in your city? What makes it special?

Answer: Yes, my favourite outdoor spot is the city park. It has beautiful gardens and a peaceful lake, making it a perfect place for a walk or picnic.

Question: What's a sport you enjoy watching? Why do you find it interesting?
Answer: I enjoy watching tennis. I find the skill and strategy of the players fascinating, and the matches are often very exciting.

Question: How do you like to relax after a busy week?
Answer: After a busy week, I like to relax by having a movie night at home or going for a gentle walk in the neighbourhood.

Question: Can you tell me about a cultural event or tradition that's unique to your country?
Answer: A unique cultural event in my country is the Midsummer celebration. We have bonfires, traditional music, and dance to celebrate the longest day of the year.

Question: What's a hobby you enjoy that helps you unwind?
Answer: A hobby that helps me unwind is gardening. It's calming to be in nature, and taking care of plants is rewarding.

Question: Can you describe an interesting historical landmark you've visited?
Answer: An interesting historical landmark I've visited is the Tower of London. It has a rich history and is famous for its role in British royal history.

Question: What's a personal goal you have for this year?
Answer: A personal goal I have for this year is to improve my public speaking skills. I plan to join a local club to practice and gain confidence.
Question: What's a recent movie you enjoyed and why?
Answer: I recently watched "Little Women" and really enjoyed it. The acting was superb and the story was both heartwarming and empowering.

Question: Can you describe a special holiday memory?
Answer: A special holiday memory for me was a Christmas when my whole family gathered at my grandparents' house. We shared stories, ate a lot of delicious food, and played games.

Question: What's your favourite season of the year and why?
Answer: My favourite season is autumn. I love the colourful leaves, the cooler weather, and the cozy feeling of the season.

Question: Do you have a favourite park or nature area you like to visit?
Answer: Yes, there's a national park near my city that I love. It has beautiful hiking trails and stunning natural scenery.

Question: What's a hobby or activity that you find relaxing?
Answer: I find painting very relaxing. It's a great way to express myself creatively and unwind at the same time.

Question: How do you prefer to celebrate special occasions with friends?

Answer: I prefer celebrating special occasions with friends by having a potluck dinner. Everyone brings a dish, and we enjoy a variety of foods together.

Question: Can you tell me about a traditional craft or art form from your country?
Answer: A traditional craft from my country is basket weaving. It's an ancient skill that involves weaving natural materials into functional items.

Question: What's a unique or unusual pet you've seen or heard of?
Answer: A unique pet I've heard of is a sugar glider. It's a small, nocturnal, gliding possum that some people keep as a pet.

Question: Can you describe an interesting custom or celebration in your culture?
Answer: An interesting custom in my culture is the celebration of the Lunar New Year. It involves family gatherings, special meals, and giving red envelopes with money for good luck.

Question: What's a skill you would like to learn in the future?
Answer: In the future, I would like to learn how to play the piano. I've always been fascinated by the instrument and would love to play music myself.

Question: What's an interesting local custom in your area?
Answer: In my area, there's a custom of celebrating the first day of spring by planting a tree. It's a way to promote environmental awareness.

Question: Can you describe a favourite piece of art or a painting you like?
Answer: I really like Vincent van Gogh's "Starry Night." The swirling sky and bright stars create a dreamy and magical feeling.

Question: What's a memorable lesson you learned from a family member?
Answer: A memorable lesson I learned from my grandmother is to always be kind to others. She always says that kindness is the most important quality a person can have.

Question: Do you have a favourite kind of weather for outdoor activities?
Answer: My favourite weather for outdoor activities is a sunny, cool day. It's perfect for hiking or picnicking without being too hot.

Question: What's a recent personal achievement you're proud of?
Answer: A recent achievement I'm proud of is completing a half marathon. I trained for months, and crossing the finish line was an amazing feeling.

Question: How do you prefer to start your day?
Answer: I prefer to start my day with a morning jog. It energizes me and helps me clear my mind for the day ahead.

Question: Can you tell me about an unusual job or profession you know of?

Answer: An unusual job I know of is a professional tea taster. They taste different teas and help in the process of tea making and selection.

Question: What's a unique or exotic food you've tried?
Answer: A unique food I've tried is durian. It's known for its strong smell, but the taste is surprisingly sweet and creamy.

Question: Can you describe a local festival or event you enjoy?
Answer: I enjoy our local jazz festival. It's an annual event where musicians from all over come to perform. The atmosphere is always lively.

Question: What's a book or story that has influenced your thinking?
Answer: "The Little Prince" by Antoine de Saint-Exupéry has influenced my thinking. It taught me the importance of looking beneath the surface and valuing the simple things in life.

Question: What's an unusual hobby you have heard of?
Answer: An unusual hobby I've heard of is extreme ironing. People take their ironing boards to remote locations and iron clothes there. It's quite quirky!

Question: Can you describe a traditional game or sport in your country?
Answer: A traditional sport in my country is cricket. It's a game played with a bat and ball on a large field, and it's very popular, especially in summer.

Question: What's your favourite way to spend time by yourself?
Answer: My favourite way to spend time alone is by going on long walks. It helps me clear my mind and enjoy some solitude.

Question: Do you have a favourite historical figure? Who is it and why?
Answer: My favourite historical figure is Winston Churchill because of his leadership during difficult times and his ability to inspire people with his speeches.

Question: What's a recent trend or fad that you find interesting?
Answer: A recent trend I find interesting is the rise of plant-based diets. It's fascinating to see how people are adopting more sustainable eating habits.

Question: How do you like to celebrate achievements or good news?
Answer: I like to celebrate achievements by going out to dinner with friends or family. It's a nice way to share the good news and enjoy each other's company.

Question: Can you tell me about a local legend or folklore from your region?
Answer: A local legend in my region is about a ghost that supposedly haunts an old mansion. The story has been passed down for generations.

Question: What's an adventure sport you would like to try?

Answer: I would like to try paragliding. The idea of soaring through the sky and seeing the landscape from above seems thrilling.

Question: Can you describe a memorable experience you had in nature?
Answer: A memorable experience I had in nature was watching the sunrise from the top of a mountain. The view and the sense of accomplishment were incredible.

Question: What's a skill or craft you admire and would like to learn?
Answer: I admire woodworking. The ability to create beautiful and functional items from wood is a skill I would love to learn.

Question: What's an interesting tradition in your family?
Answer: In my family, we have a tradition of making homemade pizza together every Friday night. It's a fun way to start the weekend and spend quality time together

Question: Can you describe a local landmark in your city?
Answer: A local landmark in my city is the old clock tower in the town square. It's over a hundred years old and still keeps time perfectly.

Question: What's your favourite type of exercise?
Answer: My favourite type of exercise is swimming. It's a great full-body workout and it's really refreshing, especially in the summer.

Question: Do you have a favourite author or book series?

Answer: My favourite author is J.K. Rowling, and I love the Harry Potter series. The magical world she created is fascinating and the stories are very engaging.

Question: What's a hobby or activity that makes you feel creative?
Answer: Cooking makes me feel creative. I enjoy experimenting with different ingredients and creating new recipes.

Question: How do you prefer to spend a sunny day?
Answer: On a sunny day, I prefer to go to the beach or have a picnic in the park. It's nice to enjoy the good weather outdoors.

Question: Can you tell me about a memorable performance or play you've seen?
Answer: I saw a memorable performance of "The Phantom of the Opera" at a local theatre. The music and costumes were spectacular.

Question: What's an interesting fact about the wildlife in your region?
Answer: An interesting fact about the wildlife in my region is that we have a large population of deer. They can often be seen in the forests and sometimes even in backyards.

Question: Can you describe a traditional dish from your country?
Answer: A traditional dish from my country is shepherd's pie. It's a hearty meal made with minced lamb and topped with mashed potatoes.

Question: What's a skill or hobby you've always wanted to try but haven't yet?
Answer: I've always wanted to try pottery. Working with clay and creating something by hand seems both challenging and rewarding.

Question: What's an interesting custom or tradition from your country?
Answer: An interesting custom from my country is celebrating the Queen's birthday with a parade known as Trooping the Colour. It's a grand event with lots of pomp and ceremony.

Question: Can you describe a memorable trip you took as a child?
Answer: A memorable trip I took as a child was to a safari park. Seeing wild animals like lions and elephants up close was an unforgettable experience.

Question: What's your favourite way to spend time outdoors?
Answer: My favourite way to spend time outdoors is by going on nature walks. I love exploring new trails and enjoying the tranquility of the forest.

Question: Do you have a favourite museum or art gallery? What do you like about it?
Answer: My favourite museum is the Natural History Museum. I love the dinosaur exhibit and the variety of natural wonders displayed there.

Question: What's a popular sport in your country, and how is it played?

Answer: A popular sport in my country is rugby. It's a high-energy game played with an oval ball, where teams try to score points by getting the ball over the opponent's goal line.

Question: How do you like to relax after a long day?
Answer: After a long day, I like to relax by listening to music or doing some gardening. It helps me to unwind and feel peaceful.

Question: Can you tell me about a festival or celebration that's unique to your area?
Answer: A unique festival in my area is the Lantern Festival. It involves releasing lanterns into the sky, which creates a beautiful sight as they float away.

Question: What's an adventure or experience you'd like to have someday?
Answer: Someday, I'd like to go hot air ballooning. The idea of floating high above the countryside and seeing the world from a new perspective is exciting.

Question: Can you describe a traditional garment or costume from your country?
Answer: A traditional garment from my country is the kilt, a knee-length skirt-like garment worn by men. It's usually made of wool and has a tartan pattern.

Question: What's a personal challenge you've overcome recently?
Answer: A personal challenge I've recently overcome is learning to speak in public. I used to be quite nervous, but I've gained confidence through practice.

Question: What's an interesting local tradition in your community?
Answer: In my community, there's a tradition of hosting a street fair every summer. Local artisans display their crafts and there's live music and food stalls.

Question: Can you describe a memorable birthday celebration you had?
Answer: A memorable birthday I had was when I turned 18. My family surprised me with a party and my friends all came. We had a great time dancing and eating cake.

Question: What's your favourite season and how do you like to spend it?
Answer: My favourite season is spring. I love to spend it gardening and enjoying the blooming flowers and longer days.

Question: Do you have a favourite historical period? Why does it interest you?
Answer: My favourite historical period is the Renaissance. I'm fascinated by the incredible advancements in art, science, and exploration during that time.

Question: What's a sport or physical activity you recently tried?
Answer: I recently tried paddle boarding. It was challenging at first to balance, but it turned out to be a fun and relaxing way to enjoy the water.

Question: How do you like to spend a lazy afternoon?

Answer: On a lazy afternoon, I like to spend time reading a good book or watching a classic film. It's a great way to unwind and relax.

Question: Can you tell me about a unique animal native to your country?
Answer: A unique animal native to my country is the hedgehog. It's a small mammal known for its spiky coat and cute appearance.

Question: What's an adventure you'd love to go on?
Answer: I'd love to go on a safari adventure in Africa. Seeing wild animals like lions and elephants in their natural habitat would be amazing.

Question: Can you describe a traditional craft or skill from your region?
Answer: A traditional skill from my region is lace-making. It's a delicate craft that involves intricately weaving threads to create beautiful designs.

Question: What's a recent personal accomplishment that made you proud?
Answer: A recent accomplishment that made me proud was completing a photography course. I learned a lot and it's improved the quality of my photos significantly.

Question: What's an interesting piece of local history from your area?
Answer: An interesting piece of local history is that our town was a major hub during the railway expansion in the 19th century. It played a significant role in the region's development.

Question: Can you describe a favourite family recipe or dish?
Answer: A favourite family recipe is my grandmother's apple pie. It's a traditional recipe with a flaky crust and a sweet, cinnamon-infused apple filling.

Question: What's your favourite kind of weather and why?
Answer: My favourite kind of weather is a crisp autumn day. I love the cool air and the changing colours of the leaves.

Question: Do you have a favourite park or natural area you visit? What do you like about it?
Answer: My favourite natural area is the coastal path near my home. I love the sea views and the sound of the waves. It's very calming.

Question: What's a sport or physical activity you find interesting?
Answer: I find rock climbing interesting. It requires strength, strategy, and mental focus, and it seems like a rewarding challenge.

Question: How do you prefer to spend your evenings?
Answer: I prefer to spend my evenings relaxing at home, maybe watching a film or catching up on some reading.

Question: Can you tell me about a popular cultural event or festival in your country?
Answer: A popular festival in my country is the Notting Hill Carnival. It's a vibrant celebration of Caribbean culture, full of music, dance, and colourful costumes.

Question: What's an adventure sport you would love to try?
Answer: I would love to try skydiving. The thrill of jumping out of a plane and free-falling seems exhilarating.

Question: Can you describe an interesting tradition or custom you've experienced?
Answer: An interesting custom I've experienced is the Japanese tea ceremony. It's a beautiful and intricate ritual that's both calming and respectful.

Question: What's a personal goal you have for the next year?
Answer: A personal goal for the next year is to learn a new language. I'm interested in Spanish because it's widely spoken and I love the culture.

Printed in Great Britain
by Amazon

47149094R00046